THE
OF SUNDAY

by
Most Rev. Dermot Clifford, D.D.
Archbishop of Cashel & Emly

Is Sunday the Lord's Day
or just another working day?

Messenger Publications

Published by
Messenger Publications,
37, Lower Leeson Street,
Dublin 2.
Tel: 676 7491. Fax: 661 1606.

Front cover photograph:
Holy Cross Abbey, Co. Tipperary
© Department of Arts, Culture and The Gaeltacht

With ecclesiastical permission,
Dublin 1996.

ISBN 1-872245-49-8

INTRODUCTION

On the first Sunday of Advent the Church begins its celebration of a new liturgical year. Through its readings and prayers the liturgy prepares the faithful for the feast of Christmas, the second most important feast of the Church's year. The Christmas feast to celebrate the birth of Christ dates back to the fourth century. It was first introduced in Rome at the Winter Solstice on December 25th. For most Irish people it is the favourite feast. It is the family celebration. It is a time of special sharing and it has happy childhood associations for most.

But Christmas takes second place to Easter in the Church's liturgical calendar since Easter celebrates the Resurrection of Our Saviour. Easter Sunday was first celebrated around the middle of the second century, 150 AD. It may seem strange to us that for the first hundred and twenty years of Christianity there was no Easter as we know it, and no Christmas for the first three hundred years.

Was there any feast-day then in those early times? There certainly was. There was a weekly celebration. It took place on the first day of the week to commemorate the Resurrection. The day was first called 'The Lord's Day', 'Dies Dominica' in Latin, 'Dé Domhnaig' in Irish. Later on it was called Sunday. From a very early stage after the Resurrection Christ's followers came together to celebrate the Eucharist. Sunday has been termed the 'original feast'. It was very different from a Jewish Sabbath. It celebrated the new era ushered in by Christ's Resurrection. It was only after more than a century that a special Sunday was designated as Easter Sunday - the 'Sunday of Sundays' as it is sometimes called.

The Assembly

For the early Christians in Jerusalem the central part in the celebration of the Lord's Day was coming together for the Eucharist. It was the highlight of the week for them. The assembly, or meeting, could not be missed. The Christians were opposed from the beginning by the established religion. As they moved out from Jerusalem they were met by persecution. In their time of trial the weekly Eucharist proved to be a mighty source of strength and consolation. Many of them became martyrs in the early centuries.

A phrase which sums up their dependence on the Eucharistic celebration was, *Sine Dominica non possumus* - 'We would be lost only for Sunday'.

The Jews kept their Sabbath on Saturday. Sunday, the first day of the week, was a normal working day for them. So the early Christians in Jerusalem had to work on Sunday. But they assembled for the Eucharist without fail in the early morning or after work in the evening. During the persecution the Eucharist was celebrated secretly in private houses to avoid detection.

The Mass Takes Shape

By the year 150 AD the Eucharistic celebration was well developed, as shown in this account of St Justin Martyr:

On the day which is called Sunday we have a common assembly of all who live in the cities or in the outlying districts, and the memoirs of the Apostles or the writings of the Prophets are read, as long as there is time. Then, when the reader has finished, the president of the assembly verbally admonishes and invites all to imitate such examples of virtue. Then we all stand up together and offer up our prayers, and after we finish our prayers, bread and wine and water are presented. He who presides likewise offers up prayers and thanksgiving to the best of his ability, and the people express their approval by saying 'Amen'.

The Eucharistic elements are distributed and consumed by those present and to those who are absent they are sent through the deacons. The wealthy, if they wish, contribute whatever they desire, and the collection is placed in the custody of the president. With it he helps the orphans and widows, those who are needy because of sickness or any other reason, and the captives and strangers in our midst; in short, he takes care of all those in need.

You will recognise all the main parts of the Mass as we celebrate it today, including the collection! The Second Vatican Council restored many of the early Church practices, such as the *Prayers of the Faithful* and *Eucharistic Prayer II* for example, which had been lost in later centuries.

Free at Last

When the persecution of Christians ended in the early part of the fourth century with the conversion of the Roman Emperor, Constantine, Sunday was designated a holiday and many forms of work were prohibited by law. Constantine made an exception for those working in agriculture because of its vital importance for food production. Now, for the first time, it was possible for the Christian faithful to rest from physical work and to have the leisure to attend Mass and cultivate the things of the spirit.

Nevertheless, agricultural workers still found it difficult to enjoy the time and freedom to participate at Sunday Mass. Besides, when freedom to practise their religion openly was achieved, complacency gradually set in among believers. So the Church had to make attendance at Sunday Mass obligatory in the fifth century and, increasingly, it sought to prohibit work on that day. Up to that time Christians viewed attendance at Mass as a privilege rather than a duty.

Incidentally, it was around this time also that the term 'missa' was first used for the Eucharistic celebration. It had been called the 'Lord's Supper' or 'the Eucharist' in the earlier centuries. The word 'missa' came from the final words by which the celebrant 'sent' the faithful out to carry Christ's message with them and to live it out for the rest of the week.

There are therefore two separate but closely related obligations involved in the celebration of the Lord's Day. The first is the coming together for the Mass, the second is resting from work. The reason for abstaining from work on Sunday is first and foremost to ensure that time is set aside for attendance at Mass.

The Code of Canon Law sets out the two obligations very clearly and it shows how they are linked.

On Sundays and other Holydays the faithful are obliged to participate in the Mass. They are also to abstain from such work or business that would inhibit the worship to be given to God; the joy proper to the Lord's Day; or due relaxation of mind and body.

A Day of Joy and Freedom from Work

The Code of Canon Law reflects the spirit of the Second Vatican Council which, in turn, captures the enthusiasm of the early Church. In the *Constitution on the Liturgy* Vatican Council II states:

Whenever the community gathers to celebrate the Eucharist it announces the death and resurrection of the Lord; in the hope of his glorious return. The supreme manifestation of this is the Sunday assembly. This is the day of the week on which, by apostolic tradition, the Paschal Mystery is celebrated in the Eucharist in a special way.

In order that the faithful may willingly fulfil the precept to sanctify this day and understand why the Church should call them together to celebrate the Eucharist every Sunday, from the very outset of their Christian formation Sunday should be presented to them as the primordial feast day, on which, assembled together, they are to hear the Word of God and take part in the Paschal Mystery.

Moreover, any endeavour that seeks to make Sunday a genuine 'day of joy and rest from work' should be encouraged.

It is my purpose then to encourage you to make Sunday 'a genuine day of joy and rest from work.'

I am concerned that there has been some falling off in Mass attendance in the Diocese in the past year or two in particular. This fall-off is not as large here as it is in some urban areas but it must be a source of sadness and worry. Many facts have undoubtedly contributed to this decline, not least a regrettable weakening in faith and a consequent neglect of prayer. Some priests say that the introduction of Saturday evening Mass has led to a more casual approach. Young people today tend to ask, *Can I not be a good Catholic without having to go to Mass?* This is a new way of posing the question. Previous generations of teenagers would have asked, *Is it a sin to miss Mass on Sunday?*

Sunday Work

When it comes to the second question, that of Sunday rest, the situation has greatly changed. Over the past number of years The Lord's Day seems to have become an ordinary working day for a growing number of people. In town and country more and more people are engaging in business, shopping and construction, while farmers are increasingly carrying out work on the land which heretofore has been regarded as 'unnecessary servile work'. Some of the supermarkets are open for all or part of Sunday. House building, painting and decoration are in full swing even as the people make their way to Mass. There is a lively trade in second-hand furniture and an occasional farmer makes Sunday his day for spreading slurry!

Spreading slurry on a Sunday could hardly be regarded as necessary and unavoidable work. In common with many other forms of unnecessary tasks being carried out on Sundays, spreading slurry is surely out of tune with 'the joy which is proper to the feast day'. I heard a story about two genteel old ladies who had to close their windows and draw the curtains of their sitting room one fine Sunday afternoon when a neighbouring farmer appeared with his slurry spreader. 'The fellow must have no sense of the sacred,' said the first. 'And no sense of smell either,' said the other.

The Local Church

The first and more important duty on Sunday is to participate in the Mass. Mass should normally be attended with one's own community in the local church. The coming together of the local community, 'the common assembly' as Justin Martyr put it, is a very important part of the Sunday observance.

I recall how, in my young days, the men gathered outside the Church gate and talked for half an hour before the bell summoned them in five minutes before the Mass began. The women went in as they arrived and said their prayers. There might be an occasional whisper to pass on very special items of local news. After Mass the women chatted in the churchyard for a while and the men stood outside the gate again for a further half-hour before going home at their leisure. The shop across the road opened briefly after Mass and the women did a little shopping while the children bought ice-cream. The local teacher could be seen chatting with parents and the local T.D. was also regularly present.

Nowadays, most people arrive in their cars a few minutes before Mass and leave immediately afterwards. There are some who arrive a few minutes after the start of Mass and many rush away at Communion time! But the coming together of an entire local community to celebrate the Eucharist and to meet, greet and talk to each other is part and parcel of the celebration of the Sunday.

I should like to suggest that you attend Mass in your own local church when at all possible. Many people attend Mass in other parishes and never go to their local church. Sometimes these are country people who go to town in order to do their shopping after Mass. But surprisingly, there are also town people who go out the country so that they can have 'a fast Mass'. A country parish priest explained the reason for this. 'We give them good service,' he said, 'we have them out in half-an-hour!'

I am sure that if the time on the road were taken into account the forty or forty-five minute Mass in the town would prove shorter. Some people of course go to outside parishes because the standard of the liturgy, singing and preaching is better. This is more understandable. But a much better situation would be to seek to improve the liturgy in the local Church. A parish liturgical committee is the best way to improve standards of celebration.

Theology of The Mass

The celebration of the Eucharist is the true centre of the whole Christian life both for the universal Church and for the local community. The Eucharist is described by Vatican II as 'the source and summit of the whole Christian life'.

It is a celebration and a commemoration of the life-giving Passion, Death and Resurrection of Christ. An ancient hymn seeks to sum up the extraordinary mystery of the Mass in all its richness, incorporating, as it does, the Last Supper, the Cross, the Resurrection and the promise of eternal life. 'At this sacred banquet in which Christ is received, the memory of his passion is renewed, our lives are filled with grace and a promise of future glory is given to us.'

Sacrifice, Memorial and Banquet

The Second Vatican Council quotes this hymn and elaborates on it as follows:

Hence the Mass, the Lord's Supper, is at the same time and inseparably:
a sacrifice in which the sacrifice of the cross is perpetuated;
a memorial of the death and resurrection of the Lord, who said, 'Do this in memory of me';
a sacred banquet in which, through the communion of the Body and Blood of the Lord, the People of God share the benefits of the Paschal

Sacrifice, renew the New Covenant which God has made with man once for all through the Blood of Christ, and in faith and hope foreshadow and anticipate the eschatological banquet in the kingdom of the Father, proclaiming the Lord's death until his coming.

In the Mass, therefore, the sacrifice and sacred meal are part of the same mystery and they are linked together in the closest way. The Council continues:

For in the sacrifice of the Mass Our Lord is immolated when be begins to be present sacramentally as the spiritual food of the faithful under the appearances of bread and wine. It was for this purpose that Christ entrusted this sacrifice to the Church, that the faithful might share in it both spiritually, by faith and charity, and sacramentally, through the banquet of Holy Communion. Participation in the Lord's Supper is always communion with Christ offering himself for us as a sacrifice to the Father.

Christ comes to us, then, in his Word and in his Sacrament. He speaks to us in the readings, he becomes present on the altar when the bread and wine become his body and blood at the Consecration. We are thus enabled to offer Jesus to the Father, to make present the Sacrifice at Calvary and to lay hold of the graces which Our Saviour won for us on the Cross. He becomes our host, our guest and our food whenever we receive Him in Holy Communion.

Why Mass Is Offered

An old Irish hymn outlined the reasons for which we offer the Mass:

> *Ofráilimíd Íosa chun Dé a adhradh agus a mholadh,*
> *Ofráilimíd Íosa mar bhuíochas le Dia,*
> *Ofráilimíd Íosa mar cúiteamh in ár bpeacaí,*
> *Ofráilimíd Íosa chun ár riachtannais a iarradh,*
> *Ofráilimíd Íosa le taispeáint go ngráimíd Dia.*

> *We offer Jesus to worship and honour God,*
> *We offer Jesus as a thanksgiving to God,*
> *We offer Jesus in atonement for our sins,*
> *We offer Jesus to ask for our needs,*
> *We offer Jesus to show our love of God.*

The Mass In Penal Days

Down through the centuries our people have shown their faith in and their devotion to the Mass. This was especially true in the testing time of the Penal Days. This period resembles the persecutions of the early Church.

The Penal Times lasted for more than a century and a half. They began when the priests and bishops were ordered to leave the country and the Mass was banned absolutely. Very severe penalties, including forfeiture of land and possessions, awaited lay people who broke the law by sheltering priests or by attending Mass. Priests who refused to leave and got caught, were hanged, especially if they were discovered while celebrating the Holy Sacrifice. Others if they were lucky were only deported.

Our own Diocese of Cashel and Emly has many martyrs from the times of persecution. Four of them were beatified in 1992 - Dermot O'Hurley, Archbishop of Cashel; Terence Albert O'Brien, Bishop of Emly; Fr John Kearney, O.F.M., of Cashel; and Fr William Tirry, O.S.A., of Fethard. There is a further group of Irish martyrs who are next to be beatified and they include a number of lay people from Cashel. The mother of Fr John Kearney, who was martyred on the Rock of Cashel by 'Inchiquin's soldiers', is among them.

You know how our people clung to the Mass for dear life in the same way as the first century Christians did in Rome and elsewhere. They hid their priests in their homes at great personal risk and they went to Mass rocks and to other remote and secret places to attend the Holy Sacrifice.

Fr William Tirry, O.S.A., lived in one such house, that of the Everard family in Fethard. He was arrested in his vestments as he prepared to celebrate the Holy Week ceremonies there on Holy Saturday 1654 and was duly hanged in Clonmel a short time later. He was, he told the court, a religious of the Augustinian Order and a Catholic priest. It was his duty, he said, to celebrate Mass and provide the Sacraments for the Catholic people. Blessed Margaret Ball was dragged through the streets of Dublin together with a priest in his vestments after a similar raid on her home in Dublin. She died in prison some years later. Fr John Kearney told the crowd from the scaffold in Clonmel that he had been arrested, imprisoned and sentenced to hanging because he had celebrated Masses, administered the Sacraments and confirmed the people in loyalty to their Catholic faith.

These, for example, show how our ancestors viewed the Mass. Our attitude today falls badly short by comparison. We regularly see people outside our churches, chatting and smoking and displaying little or no interest in what is taking place inside the church. These sometimes claim that they are the successors of those who were on the look-out at the Mass rocks in the Penal days! My own impression is that they are getting younger and younger. But, at least, they come to the vicinity of the Church, whereas others do not bother to come at all.

I recall an amusing little incident which occurred when I was on a bus trip in Germany some years ago. I was saying Mass for the Irish group with whom I was travelling in a room off the main foyer of a hotel in Heidelberg on a Sunday morning. I had left the door of the room open deliberately in case other guests might like to join us. I had just begun the Mass when a big fellow-countryman came rushing in. He promptly banged the door closed and put his back up against it! It took generations of religious practice to produce this quintessentially Irish gesture!

Mass Houses and Chapels Allowed
As soon as the persecution eased, the Catholic faithful built Mass houses, elementary thatched buildings where they gathered on Sunday. The Blessed Sacrament could not be reserved. A little later more worthy churches or chapels were built. They still had to be erected in laneways well away from the main streets. When full freedom of worship was granted the people were more than willing to contribute to the

building of really worthy churches. Many of these churches are still with us - St John the Baptist Church in Cashel is a prime example. The generosity of our people today in contributing to the renovation and rebuilding of their parish churches is worthy of the generations who went before them. A similar faithfulness to the Sunday Mass would make this generation even more worthy of their forbears.

Mass attendance grew rapidly in the decades after Catholic Emancipation. The Sunday Mass was the centre of the week and the great majority of the people came. People missed Mass only when they were seriously ill or incapacitated. They had to travel on foot over roads and across the fields, on the Mass paths as they were called. They were often too poor to dress up. Sometimes two members of a family wore the same suit to two different morning Masses!

Towards the end of the last century Augustine Birrell identified the Mass as the crucial difference between Irish Catholicism and his own Anglican faith. Birrell was Secretary to Ireland until the 1916 Rising led to his dismissal. He was a devout Anglican and a writer of note. Here is what he said: 'It is the Mass that matters, it is the Mass that makes the difference, so hard to define, so subtle it is, yet so perceptible between a Catholic country and a Protestant one, between Dublin and Edinburgh, between Harve and Cromer.'

The Mass is essentially the same whether it is celebrated in a country kitchen in Fethard or in St Peter's Basilica in Rome. In an account by Archbishop Rinuccini of his first day in Ireland he tells how he said Mass in Kenmare on a kitchen table on which men had played cards and drank beer the night before. Older people will recall the Mass in the Phoenix Park at the Eucharistic Congress in 1932, while the younger generations will remember the Papal Mass in Galway in 1979 as memorable celebrations. But every Mass is the re-enactment of the Last Supper on Holy Thursday and the self-offering of Our Lord on Mount Calvary on Good Friday.

Saturday Evening Mass
The Church has in later years extended the time during which it is permissible to celebrate Sunday Mass. It can now take place on Saturday evening whereas previously it could only be celebrated on Sunday morning. The latest time for Mass until Vatican II was midday. This change is in recognition of the fact that the Sunday begins at sun-down on the previous evening as was the rule with the Jewish Sabbath and indeed still is. It gives a much greater opportunity to individuals and to families to get to Mass. It has to be said that our people have become very attached to the Saturday evening Mass since it was introduced in 1982. An estimated one third of our Mass-going people now come to it. It has to be said, also, that the Saturday evening Mass is one which is attended very devoutly by the faithful. A very high proportion of young people prefer this Saturday evening Mass.

As against this, however, it has to be said that it is difficult to realise that Saturday evening is the beginning of a new week. It can be a bit of a rush after a day's work on the farm or in the shop. For the priest it can sometimes be a bit of a rush from a wedding reception.

Responses to Survey

When a sample of our people were asked in a survey sometime ago to state why they went on Saturday evening rather than on Sunday their replies were interesting:

'To have a lie on in bed on Sunday', was the most frequent reason given. This response tended to come from younger people who stay out late on Saturday nights. This was the reply from almost a third (32%) of those interviewed.

The second most frequent reason given was that Saturday evening was 'more convenient'. This group included more women than men. This response was given by 30% of the sample.

'To be able to have Sunday free', was the reason given by 14%.

The fourth reason given was, 'It suits my lifestyle.' Here it is the men who were in the majority, while the young generation also figured (16%).

'I work on Sunday' (8%).

'So I can relax on Sunday morning' (5%).

'It is now a habit' (4%).

'I have to get the dinner early on Sunday' (4%). There was not a single male, or married one for that matter, in this group. Obviously any males who cook the dinner do so later in the day!

'I can only get a lift on Saturday evening' (4%).

'It is handier to have it over with on Saturday evening' (3%).

'I get more from Mass when I don't have to rush home to prepare meals' (1%).

'I have to study on Sunday' (1%, all girls).

'I sing with the folk group at Saturday evening Mass' (1%, all girls!).

'I play sport on Sunday morning' (1%, all boys) .

Other or no particular reason (1%). Some gave more than one reason.

Reflections on Survey

One would be tempted to say that the motives of the Saturday evening Mass-goers are not the most edifying! Spending most of Sunday in bed is scarcely a commendable way of celebrating the Resurrection! Personal convenience and lifestyle are obviously high priorities today. Of course, if one were to ask why people chose later or earlier Masses on Sunday, a similar set of responses might well be given. The respondents were not asked why they went to Mass, only why they chose Saturday evening over Sunday. It may be that shyness prevented people from expressing their very personal reasons to strangers.

I worry a little about the long-term effect of attending Saturday evening Mass only and never coming on Sunday. Does it affect the way in which they spend Sunday? In the old days Saturday night was the night for going to Confession and it was the night people washed, shaved, and polished their shoes. 'Saturday's splash for Sunday's dash' was how it was described.

It was the night the man of the house took down his razor and shaved with solemn ceremony. I recall a Saturday night in my childhood when an elderly man who came to work with us set up his basin, soap, towel, razor, mirror and a lighted candle on the kitchen table. As he was about to start my younger brother enquired, 'Daddy, is he going to say Mass?'

Country people dressed up on Sunday morning after they had tended the cows and looked after other necessary chores. When they came back from Mass they relaxed, had their dinner and went to games or visited relatives or neighbours. The woman of the house sat down and enjoyed the peace and quiet of Sunday afternoon. The working clothes were only put on again for milking in the evening. One wonders if, for many people, the Sunday clothes go on at any time on Sunday anymore? A man in his working clothes is almost certain to see some job which needs to be done. Then, before he knows it, he is on the tractor. He is in 'working mode'. Maybe this goes some way to explain the growth in Sunday work in the country in the past few years.

Social Importance of Sunday

In my school days we studied an essay entitled, *Sir Roger de Coverley in Church*. It was written by Joseph Addison. Sir Roger was a good natured but somewhat eccentric squire or landlord. Addison used him to expound his own ideas about Sunday. He held that the weekly gathering of the parishioners had a very important social as well as religious purpose. Getting dressed up, meeting neighbours, discussing the local news and listening to the readings and the sermon were all healthy for mind, body and soul. 'Sunday clears away the rust of the whole week', he said.

In addition, Addison noted an amusing eccentricity of Sir Roger's:

> *He will suffer nobody to sleep in the Church besides himself; for if by chance he has been surprised into a short nap at sermon, upon recovering out of it he stands up and if he see anybody else nodding, either wakes them up himself or sends his servants to them.*

Addison went so far as to say that a community without this weekly gathering would be in danger of becoming 'uncivilised' and even 'barbaric'.

Less Respect for God and Man

He wrote over three hundred years ago but there is ample evidence in our own country today to suggest that there are a number of people who do not respect God or man any more. They ignore the Ten Commandments: 'Thou shalt not kill', 'Thou shalt not steal', 'Thou shalt not commit adultery'. There are daily accounts of murder, rape, robbery, drug seizures, punishment beatings and other serious crimes in our national and local media.

I believe that when large numbers of people ignore the first three Commandments relative to the respect which is due to God, it is inevitable that they will show less and less respect for the rights of their neighbour also.

There is a cruelty, unimaginable some years ago, in many of the crimes today. This stems from a lack of respect for God in the first place and for fellow human beings in the second. It is scarcely a coincidence that increased serious crime has occurred simultaneously with a decline in religious practice. This is the published view of a high-ranking Officer of *an Garda Síochana*. It is also very interesting that some commentators who have advocated radical social changes for many years, have recently begun to express anxiety about the future of Irish society if it continues to become more and more secular and the influence of religion declines.

Unnecessary Servile Work

In earlier times the term 'unnecessary servile work' was used to describe the kind of work which was forbidden on Sunday. This concerned heavy physical labour which was not vital and could be left for the other six days of the week. Some tasks such as tending animals were called 'necessary servile work' and were permitted. On occasion, during a wet summer, the saving of crops was allowed.

From the time of Constantine, the Catholic Church obliged those who engaged in heavy physical work to rest from it on Sunday in order to have the time to attend Mass and to refresh mind and body. It had the labourer's physical, mental and spiritual good in mind. The majority of the faithful down through the centuries were serfs, servants and labourers. The Church stressed the duty of employers to free their workers on Sunday.

The Importance of Leisure

Leisure is very important for health. Leisure is actually more in tune with our spiritual nature than work.

Work, while enabling us to cooperate in God's creative plan is, nonetheless, burdensome and a consequence of our sinful state. Leisure, on the other hand, opens the human spirit to the religious, the cultural and the social sides of our nature.

One of the first socialists, a Frenchman named Pierre Proudhon, wrote a pamphlet on the celebration of Sunday. He stressed its social importance as follows:

One day in the week servants regained the dignity of human beings and stood again on a level with their masters.

He went on to argue that proper rest and leisure time should be a higher priority for workers than higher wages. Double pay would not compensate for the loss of Sunday. Proudhon grew up in the country and had very happy childhood memories of Sunday.

Of primary importance in the notion of leisure is divine worship. The first feast-days were always religious in character. The Greek philosopher Plato expressed this as follows:

But the gods, taking pity on mankind born to work, laid down the succession of recurring Feasts to restore them from their fatigue so that nourishing themselves in festive companionship with the gods they should again stand upright and erect.

The Irish word for feast-day is 'feile', which also came to denote the festival and celebration which accompanied the feast day of a particular season or saint. The word 'culture' comes from 'cultus' in Latin, meaning the divine worship.

Sabbatarianism

Sunday rest sometimes suggests an empty, dreary and boring day. In countries the Reformation, like England and Scotland, the Sunday rest meant abstaining not only from work but also from all forms of sport and entertainment. This strict observance is called 'Sabbatarianism'. It takes its origin from the Jewish laws which forbade almost all activity on the Sabbath. The Irish people tended to ignore the English laws against Sunday games but hurling suffered because of them. The modern Seventh Day Adventists are also of this strict sabbatarian view.

You recall how the Pharisees protested to the Apostles for plucking grains of corn and eating them on the Sabbath and how they also attacked Our Lord for healing the sick. Jesus rejected this very rigid observance, although he attended the synagogue on the Sabbath. His verdict, 'The Sabbath was made for man, not man for the Sabbath', was a call for common sense and for freedom to engage in good neighbourly activity on the Sabbath.

In the not too distant past, Sunday golf was not permitted in Scotland. When a famous professional at St Andrew's was queried on it he replied, 'Even if *you* don't need the rest the greens do!' A spokesperson for the Seventh Day Adventists, who forbid all forms of entertainment, was contacted by the media about the prohibition on the Sabbath day itself. The spokesperson promptly replied, 'We don't release statements on the Sabbath!' When it comes to Sunday observance it is more difficult to strike the happy medium than to go to the extremes.

In the Catholic view, wholesome leisure activities are not only allowed, but they are encouraged as long as they do not interfere with religious observance. This was the position adopted by Dr Croke who is credited by Brother Liam Ó Caithnia in his book *Scéal na h-Iomána* with sounding the death-knell of sabbatarianism in Ireland through his support for Gaelic games and pastimes on Sunday afternoon.

Leisure activities can range from watching television, listening to music, visiting or entertaining friends or relatives to actual participation in sport or in voluntary work. A recent book on leisure lists ten main forms of leisure activities. It names religious practice as one.

A modern writer, Brian Wilson, describes the social change which has been taking place in recent times:

> *Instead of work, family life, education and religious practice, the operation of law and custom and recreation all being part of each other and affecting everyone in more or less self-sufficient close-knit small communities, as occurred in large measure in all pre-modern societies, we have highly specialised places, times, resources and personnel involvement in each of these areas of social life, and their efficiency and viability has depended on this process of specialisation. In the past, religion*

was a primary socialising agency of people, teaching them not only new rituals but something of the seriousness of eternal verities. Today, religion has come to be associated much more as one among a number of leisure activities, it exists in the area of free choice of the use of time, energy and the use of wealth in which the end products of the economy are marketed for consumers.

Consumer Choice

We are in the age of consumer choice. Many different interest groups compete for our time and money. Religious observance is one of many choices open to us. While it may be legitimate to classify religious practice as a leisure activity, the Sunday observance should be the most important event of the week for the faithful. All other weekend activities should give way to it.

The essence of leisure is the enjoyment of an activity which is freely chosen and is not carried out for payment. Sometimes I hear Gaelic players express the view that if only they were paid for playing the game they love they would have the best of all worlds. However, I believe that as soon as one is paid to play it becomes a duty; it becomes work, and consequently a good deal of the enjoyment is gone. One *has* to play, that is what one is paid to do. This constitutes the difference between work and leisure.

When it comes to the distribution of work, there are the two extremes. There are those who have too much of it, who are always on the job and never let up on Sunday or Monday. They never have a minute to spare. Work is their only interest. They cannot bear to be idle. Their preoccupation with work brings to mind the lines:

What is this life if, so full of care,
we have no time to stand and stare.

What such driven people often fail to realise is that they would probably get far more done if they took a break one day a week! Sunday could be a godsend for them.

When Leisure Loses Its Meaning
At the other extreme are those who cannot find work. They have no job to fill their day. They often feel rejected and so their self esteem suffers. When one does not have work, leisure can lose its meaning.

Leisure and sporting organisations should try to ensure that the unemployed become more involved in sports, hobbies and other interests, thus giving their lives greater structure and meaning.

Not surprisingly, the unemployed sometimes tend to become discouraged. They cease to play a part in the social life of their communities. This is due, in part, to lack of money, but perhaps they just do not have the heart. This sad development can lead some of the unemployed to opt out of Mass attendance. And this is a great pity.

I should like to take this opportunity to invite those who do not enjoy their right to work to come and join the community at Sunday Mass. The fact that society has failed or neglected them is not a valid reason to fight shy of the Mass.

Liberal or Light Work

The Church's traditional prohibition of 'unnecessary servile work' was a great safeguard against the exploitation of workers. The opposite to servile work is called 'liberal work'. This refers to intellectual work, writing, playing musical instruments, art work and the like. This work was always allowed on Sunday.

The distinction between servile and liberal work is not easily made today. I think the deciding factor in relation to what is and what is not permissible on Sunday is twofold. Is the work done for financial gain and, if so, is it essential?

The factors previously mentioned are also still important, of course. Does the work interfere with Sunday observance - one's own or that of others? Does it interfere with family commitments? Another approach might be, that, regardless of its nature, people should abstain on Sunday from the work they have been doing on the other days of the week.

'Liberal' work includes people in offices and in all other non-manual areas. People who work in these areas can be under a great deal of pressure, too. They need a rest, a break and a change just as much as those who do heavy manual work. Sunday should be the day which gives them these. It should be a day that is 'different'. It *is* special, but if Sunday is to remain the Lord's Day and not become an ordinary working day the present trend will have to be checked and checked soon. Too much will be lost if we stand by and allow market forces to sweep away our long established traditions.

The Jewish religious leaders found it difficult to keep their people from trading on the Sabbath. Foreigners would come to Jerusalem and set up a market on the day of rest. The Jews found it very difficult to resist a good bargain! The local traders, not wishing to let it go with the foreigners, set up their own stalls. At one stage Nehemiah, their civil and religious leader, put a stop to the market by ordering the gates of Jerusalem to be closed during the Sabbath! So 'Sunday trading' has its roots in the Old Testament!

Responsibilty of Employers

I stated earlier that the main reason for abstaining from work on a Sunday was to provide time for Mass attendance. This applies in a particular way to employers. They must ensure that their employees are given adequate time to attend Mass - I speak here of employers whose service of the public demands that they work on Sundays: in the service industries such as health care, security, transport, hotels, restaurants, public houses and so on. These and others of a similar nature must make sure to give their employees sufficient free time to go to Mass. They should, if possible, also see to it that individuals do not have to work every Sunday. A rota system solves this problem.

There is a danger of stress in all occupations nowadays and continued stress can lead to what is called 'burn-out'. The weekly break can be very helpful in coping with stress, especially if it is spent with the family. The danger of taking the problems of the job back home is a very real one. A parent can then be too preoccupied to play his or her part in the life of the home. The ability to switch off from the job is vital both for the worker and for the family. On Sunday one can escape from the job for long enough to recuperate.

Leisure and Religious Duty

It is not only work which can interfere with Sunday worship. Leisure activities can also prevent people, especially young people, from attending Sunday Mass. At the present time there is intense competition between different sporting organisations for young people. There is football, handball, hurling, soccer, camogie, rugby and cycling - all in competition for the young. A boy of fourteen played fifty-six competitive games last summer.

I have the greatest admiration for the adults who give their free time gratis and for nothing to transport young people and to train them in skills and in sportsmanship. But a situation exists in some parishes where there are games both on Saturday evening and on Sunday morning at the same times as the parish Masses.

A game or a practice session can be in progress as the people are on their way to Mass. This is a case where leisure activities conflict with the primary purpose of Sunday which is, as I have said, Mass attendance without distractions or counter attractions.

Young people should not be placed in a position where they have to choose between playing a game or going to Mass.

A Satisfactory Agreement

I appeal to the priests, to the parents and to the organisers of the different sports to work out a week-end timetable which ensures that young people are not prevented from attending Mass because of field games or other leisure activities.

There was a time when our priests were involved more in the running of games, athletics and other leisure pursuits. But I know that many of them take an active interest in leisure activities. In any case, I hope that the priests can come to a satisfactory agreement with the sports organisations to ensure that games times and Mass times do not coincide.

In the days of the fairs long ago, the following motion was put to a County Council by one of the members: 'If fairs collide they should collide at a distance'. I sincerely hope that games and Masses do not 'collide' at all!

Dr Croke's Appeal

I should like in this context to recall a request which my predecessor Dr Croke, first patron of the *Gaelic Athletic Association,* made to the *National Convention of the G.A.A.* held in Thurles in January 1888:

> *I am assured on reliable authority that several of the young athletes who are engaged in Sunday sports, especially when they have to go*

> *a good way from home, habitually miss Mass in*
> *consequence and that such sports possess so*
> *great an attraction now for a still more juvenile*
> *portion of our people that instead of attending*
> *their catechism classes in Church after last*
> *Mass, as they ought to do, they accompany*
> *their adult friends and neighbours to the hurl-*
> *ing and football games - thus greatly displeas-*
> *ing their parents and doing no small harm to*
> *themselves.*

Dr Croke went on to suggest that games which involved long distance travel should not take place on Sundays or holydays of obligation. The parish or interparish competition should not take place until after 2.00 pm on Sundays. This was, of course, in the days before the motor car, the Saturday evening Mass and the advent of television.

I know that our sporting organisations generally are very conscious of the importance of the Mass and go to considerable trouble to ensure that their players have the opportunity to attend when playing away from home. I realise also that Sunday would be a much less enjoyable day for young and old alike were it not for the games and other cultural activities.

On the special Sunday devoted to vocations this year, one of our parish priests asked an altar boy if he had ever thought of becoming a priest. 'I did', said the ten-year-old, 'but as I am into set-dancing and all the competitions are on Sunday I could not manage the two'. So, it is not only field games which clash with Sunday observance!

Spiritual Reading

Sunday worship should not end with the attendance at Mass. The day should include the time and the space for prayer and reflection, and for reading something with a religious content.

Away from the hustle and bustle of the week-day world of work or school, people should be more open to the spiritual. They should be more aware of the presence of the Lord and think about his goodness and pray to him for their needs in the week ahead. This could be done in the home or in a walk in the country or sitting in the back garden.

A farmer told me lately, 'I like to have a good read on a Sunday'. What did he read? The Sunday papers. There is very little spiritual content in them, I have to say. In so far as religion is ever mentioned, it is usually in the context of controversy.

You need to seek some 'spiritual vitamins or supplements' from the Catholic press if you are not to be spiritually undernourished. I recommend that you take and read a Catholic weekly paper. My own choice is the *Irish Catholic* but there are a number of others which are also suitable. Sunday would be an ideal day for such reading.

The Family Day

Sunday should, of course, be very much a family day. It is often the only day on which the family members spend time together. It is important to set time aside for conversation, meals, or an outing. During the week parents and children go their different ways, to work or to school. The home can become like a pitstop in a motor-rally as teenagers rush in and out! Sunday provides the opportunity to be together in a relaxed atmosphere.

I saw a film on the life of the late Bing Crosby recently. As you will know, he entertained millions through films, radio, television and records. His song, *A White Christmas,* is an all-time favourite. The public loved his relaxed manner. When he was not working at his music and singing, he was playing golf - very often for charity. Like many sporting people in this area he kept race horses and was seen regularly at the races. The only problem was that he was hardly ever at home. His wife and family saw very little of him. When they did, he was, it seems, a very strict and sometimes a harsh disciplinarian.

Sunday Shopping

It it more important now than ever it was to work at building harmony and peace in the home. Sunday provides the opportunity for doing so.

Those supermarkets which open on Sundays prevent their employees from being with their families. There is very little need for such opening since there are six other days in the week, and evening and night opening are now common. There seems to be little reason to suggest that the general public, the customers, could not fit in their shopping on the week days and so keep Sunday free from buying and selling. Most European countries do not have Sunday shopping. It must be acknowledged that some of the supermarket chains do not open on Sundays and these deserve great credit when their competitors are trading. Legislation here to raise Sunday pay sufficiently high to make trading unprofitable may be the only way to solve the problem of Sunday trading.

It will be necessary, on occasion, to buy some items at the corner shop which is usually a family business and gives a service after Mass. One sees the larger shops open on the Sundays before Christmas and then for three or four days after Christmas Day one meets old people searching in vain to buy a loaf of bread in town! I appeal to you, never make Sunday your shopping day.

As regards window shopping on Sundays - is it a legitimate pastime? Yes, but the temptation to get a bargain may prove too strong to resist!

The question should be: *Is Sunday the Lord's Day or is it just another shopping day?* We are in serious danger of forgetting or ignoring the Lord in favour of consumer goods. Jesus told us, 'Where your treasure is there will your heart be also'.

Sunday Prayer

The family should say some prayers together every day but particularly on the Lord's Day. The Rosary is a wonderful family prayer. It has a very long tradition in Ireland since the Penal Days when it was a substitute for the Mass if a priest could not be found. The Irish name for the Rosary was *An Paidrín Pairteach* - The Shared Prayer.

Other prayers can be excellent also. I sent a prayer leaflet to every home in the Diocese sometime ago. Remember, *The family that prays together stays together.*

Sunday is also a very suitable day for visiting relatives, neighbours and friends. The elderly and the sick are especially in need of a visit since they are not always able to get about. They will usually appreciate this kindness and it brightens up their day. Life can be lonely for them as nowadays everybody is seemingly too busy to talk and listen to them.

It is sometimes suggested that in the modern world with its wide variety of working hours, flexi-time and so on, every person should be free to select his or her day off - one day being as good as the next. One could, the argument goes on, choose the day most suitable to oneself and go to a week-day morning or evening Mass and choose any day of the week as your Sabbath. The problem here is that the community dimension of Sunday would then be lost. More importantly, Sunday is the day on which the Lord's Resurrection is celebrated. It is the first day of the week in every sense.

A small number of people still attend Devotions and Benediction on Sunday evening. It is their way of crowning the Lord's Day. Years ago a much larger congregation attended. There were sodalities and confraternities which swelled the crowd regularly. On the evening of Munster Finals in Thurles a regular attender at Benediction was the late Christy Ring. He came to thank the Lord at the end of an often tumultuous day at the Stadium. The Sunday evening Benediction fell victim to television but it was and can still be a very fitting way to end the Sunday.

Importance of Practice

Young people sometimes ask the question: 'Can I be a good Catholic and not go to Mass?' My short answer is, 'You can for about three weeks and then your faith will begin to weaken.' If I were to ask the question 'Can you be a good hurler and never practise, or, can you be a good dancer and never dance, what would you answer?' Can you be a good member of the local youth club having given up going to the meetings and organised functions? In some organisations those who miss three consecutive meetings without a sufficient reason lose their membership automatically.

The Mass is *unique* as I hope I have shown. I would urge young people to learn about it and to begin to appreciate its incalculable value and its depths of mystery. Merely to say, *I get nothing out of it,* and make no effort to get to know more about it is to fail to accept the most precious gift on earth.

The early Christians would never have asked that question. The people who went before us and the older generation today would find it difficult to see how one could deliberately miss Mass and still claim to be a good Catholic. But young people today do not take kindly to doing things because the Church obliges them or their parents order them. They need to *feel* that they are getting something out of doing things. But to get anything out, we must first put something in. In this case the Mass will richly repay some serious study. That, I guarantee.

Special Appeal

I should like to conclude with a word of praise to all who are faithful to the Sunday and to Saturday evening Mass. You have fulfilled your duty faithfully week after week, year after year.

I should like to make a very special plea to people who have given up coming to Sunday Mass. You are missed. This congregation, the Church, is the poorer for your absence. I invite you to rejoin your neighbours at the weekly celebration. A very good time to return is Christmas. Come to the Mass at Christmas and then continue in the New Year. You will soon feel at home again. You will feel better and more at ease with your conscience and with your family. I appeal earnestly not to allow any old hurt or recent scandal to keep you away from your greatest source of grace as a baptised Catholic. In the words of the early Christians again, 'Without the Sunday we would be lost'.

Church Gate Collections

Many people today complain about Church gate collections. While most of them are for good causes, people feel that there are too many of them and that the collectors can sometimes impede and embarrass them.

On a Holyday evening I heard two women on the footpath discussing whether or not there was an evening Mass in the Cathedral. 'There can't be', one of them concluded, 'there is no one collecting at the gate.' A country man who was suffering from donation fatigue at the church gate declared to his friends, 'Twould be cheaper to bring the priest to the house.'

As you are aware, a permit to take up a collection comes from the Garda authorities. There is a strict rule about keeping collection boxes 50 feet from either side of every church gate. I appeal to those who collect to keep the law. Many organisations involved in laudable humanitarian, recreational and other community activities now adopt more novel and, I believe, more profitable means of raising funds.

CONCLUSION

I have, I hope, dealt with the two principal aspects of Sunday, attendance at Mass and the abstention from work and from commerce. Sunday not only celebrates the Resurrection of Our Lord, it also looks to our own resurrection and to our final coming to Christ, the 'King of the Sunday', Rí an Domhnaigh as the Irish people called Our Lord. Our ancestors had a special prayer to greet the King of the Sunday:

Fáilte romhat a Rí an Domhnaigb,
A Mhic na hÓighe a rinne an Aiséirí.

Welcome, King of the Sunday,
the Son of the Virgin who rose from the dead.

Another poem welcomes the Sunday itself -
Dé do bheatha cughainn a Dhomhnaigh bheannaithe.

We bid you welcome, blessed Sunday,
a fine and joyful day after the week,
a fine and lovely day to speak to Christ.
Stir your feet and make your way to Mass.
Stir your heart and drive from it all spite.
Stir your lips and speak words of blessing.
Look up and see the Son of the Blessed Nurse,
the Son of the Virgin, for it was he who
redeemed us;
may we be his in life and in death.

If we are to be his in life we must get our priorities right. On the day he calls us to be his in death we will have to drop everything, and leave our work, our houses, our land, our money and all our most treasured possessions.

For Augustine Birrell the thought that the books he had collected over a lifetime would be taken from their shelves 'by rude hands' and sold off, was the saddest thing about death. 'Fool that I was to call anything mine!', he wrote.

To drop everything on Sunday could be a weekly preparation for this final renunciation. *The King of the Sunday* once asked his followers:

What then will anyone gain by winning the whole world and forfeiting his life?